Financial Analysis and Time Value of Money

Personal Financial Decisions

Juan R. Castro, Ph.D.

Professor of Finance and Economics

WELCOME

If you are interested in learning how to evaluate the performance of your own company or analyze the performance of a corporation from which you want to buy stocks or bonds, this book will guide you on how to do it. If you want to learn about present and future values and how to apply them for portfolio investments and retirement, this book will be a great resource for you.

This book will teach you how to evaluate a company or an investment. This is a practical book in which you can learn about financial ratios and compounding. It provides several examples that enhance the understanding of financial analysis and time value of money. This book covers financial analysis and time value of money. Financial analysis is the process of evaluating personal funds, businesses, projects, budgets, and other finance-related transactions to determine their performance and suitability.

The time value of money (TVM) is the concept that the money you have now is worth more than the identical sum in the future due to its potential earning capacity. Time value of money is based on the idea that people would rather have money today than in the future. Given that money can earn compound interest, it is more valuable in the present rather than the future.

This core principle of finance holds that provided money can earn interest, any amount of money is worth more the sooner it is received. TVM is also sometimes referred to as present discounted value. The formula for computing time value of money consider the payment now, the future value, the interest rate, and the time frame. The number of compounding periods during each time frame is an important determinant in the time value of the money formula as well.

In this book, you will learn the following content:
- Company analysis
- Financial ratios,
- Personal financial ratios

- Balance Sheet
- Income statement
- Earnings per Share
- Price- Earnings ratio
- Book Value
- Personal Financial Ratios
- Savings ratio
- Debt to income ratio
- Liquidity ratio
- Profit Margins
- Future Value
- Present Value
- Annuities
- Amortizations

Acknowledgments

After teaching finance and personal finance for more than 24 years in college and with the community, I have learned to recognize how many people have invested in my personal education and realizations. I am grateful for the many of my students and peers who have significantly contributed to this book by sharing their expertise, classroom discussions, written assignments, and general advice. I particularly want to thank my wife Lizete and my children Juan, Esther, and Daniel. They have been a motivating force to finish this work. I definitively want to thank God for allowing me enough time to work on the things I love in my life.

About the Author

A seasoned and experienced professor, Dr. Juan R. Castro, has a Ph.D. in financial economics and has been teaching finance, economics, and personal finance for more than 24 years. He has been teaching personal finance and financial literacy in English and Spanish in several universities, churches, communities, and countries. Dr. Castro is a Fulbright Scholar, former UNDP consultant, and has experience in banking as vice president of risk management. He has written books in Principles of Quantitative Finance, Personal Finance Planning, Financial Literacy in English and Spanish, Dollarization, and Financial Cases.

Table of Contents

1: Financial Statements

6	Introduction
8	Financial Statements
11	*Balance Sheet*
16	Stockholder's Equity
20	**Income Statement**
25	Net Income
26	**Statement of Cash Flows**

2: Financial Ratios

34	Earnings per Share
35	Price to Sales Ratio
36	Dividend per Share
36	Payout Ratio
37	Book Value per Share
38	Net Profit Margin
38	Operating Margin
39	Savings Ratio
39	Debt to Income Ratio
40	Housing Cost Ratio
40	Total Debt Ratio
41	**Liquidity Ratios**
46	Gross Profit Margin
47	Net Profit Margin

3: Time Value of Money

62	What is Time Value?
63	Future Value
64	Present Values
66	Future Values - applications
67	Annuities
67	Future Value of an Ordinary Annuity
68	Future Value of an Annuity Due
70	Finding the Interest Rate, I
70	Finding the Number of Years, N
71	Future Value of an Uneven Cash Flow Stream
72	Growing Annuities
74	Amortization Tables

4: Conclusion

76	Conclusions
77	Video Practices for Financial Analysis
78	References

Financial Decisions and Time Value of Money

Introduction

If you can read a nutrition label or a baseball box score, you can learn to read basic financial statements. If you can follow a recipe or apply for a loan, you can learn basic accounting. The basics aren't difficult and they aren't rocket science.

This brochure is designed to help you gain a basic understanding of how to read financial statements. Just as a CPR class teaches you how to perform the basics of cardiac pulmonary resuscitation, this brochure will explain how to read the basic parts of a financial statement. It will not train you to be an accountant (just as a CPR course will not make you a cardiac doctor), but it should give you the confidence to be able to look at a set of financial statements and make sense of them.

In this book, we are going to be discussing some basics of company's financials.

In a previous book from the same author (see Foundations of Risk and Return), we have been discussing the personal and statistical side of finance. Now that you have the basic knowledge of your own finances, we want to discuss how to view a company's. After this module, you will be able to help yourself in building your financial portfolio. You will not have to rely just on the information a financial representative provides you.

In the first section of this book, you will learn about the basic financial statements. Public companies are required to put these types of statements out to the public. We will be focusing on a Balance Sheet and Income statement.

In the second section, we will be discussing the different types of financial ratios that analysts use to analyze companies. You may be wondering why you should know about these ratios. After studying this book, you will be able to perform a basic financial analysis of a company yourself. You will use this type of financial analysis when you are preparing yourself to invest in a company. This section will also talk about the limitations of the ratios. The ratios are very helpful but do not always tell the whole story.

The last section we will be discussing is about time value of money. Time value of money will help you look at a company's stock or investment and predict the worth of the investment. You will be able to plan our investments using this information. Using this type of information will again help you when you invest to build your portfolio.

1: Financial Statements

What are Financial Statements?

Financial Statements *are records that indicate an individual's, organization, or business' financial status.* If you can read a nutrition label or a baseball box score, you can learn to read basic financial statements. If you can follow a recipe or apply for a loan, you can learn basic accounting. The basics aren't difficult and they aren't rocket science.

There are three main financial statements. They are:

1. Balance Sheets
2. Income Statements
3. Cash Flow Statements

Balance Sheets *show what a company owns and what it owes at a fixed point in time.* **Income Statements** *show how much money a company made and spent over a period of time.* **Cash Flow Statements** *show the exchange of money between a company and the outside world also over some time.* A financial statement records that outline the financial activities of a business, an individual, or any other entity. Financial statements are meant to present the financial information of the entity in question as clearly and concisely as possible for both the entity and for readers. Financial statements for businesses usually include income statements, balance sheets, statements of retained earnings and cash flows, as well as other possible statements.

> **Financial statements are meant to present the financial information of the entity in questions as clearly and concisely as possible**

It is a standard practice for businesses to present financial statements that adhere to Generally Accepted Accounting Principles (GAAP), *to maintain continuity of information and presentation across international borders.* As well, financial statements are often audited by government agencies, accountants, firms, etc. to ensure accuracy and for tax, financing, or investing purposes. Financial statements are integral to ensuring accurate and honest accounting for businesses and individuals alike. Personal Financial Statements are documents or spreadsheets outlining an individual's financial position at a given point in time. A personal financial statement will typically include general information about the individual, such as name and address, along with a breakdown of their total assets and liabilities. Assets would include any account balances in checking or savings accounts, retirement account balances, trading accounts, and real estate. Liabilities would cover items such as credit card balances, loans, and mortgages.

This is an example of a personal Financial Statement provided for free by the U.S. Small Business Administration, SBA. As you can see, it goes through every point mentioned above that is a part of a good Financial Statement.

Read the Footnotes

A horse called "Read The Footnotes" ran in the 2004 Kentucky Derby. He finished seventh, but if he had won, it would have been a victory for financial literacy proponents everywhere. It's so important to read the footnotes. The footnotes to financial statements are packed with information. Here are some of the highlights:

- Significant accounting policies and practices – Companies are required to disclose the accounting policies that are most important to the portrayal of the company's financial condition and results. These often require management's most difficult, subjective, or complex judgments.
- Income taxes – The footnotes provide detailed information about the company's current and deferred income taxes. The information is broken down by level – federal, state, local, and/or foreign, and the main items that affect the company's effective tax rate are described.
- Pension plans and other retirement programs – The footnotes discuss the company's pension plans and other retirement or post-employment benefit programs. The notes contain specific information about the assets and costs of these programs, and indicate whether and by how much the plans are over- or under-funded.
- Stock options – The notes also contain information about stock options granted to officers and employees, including the method of accounting for stock-based compensation and the effect of the method on reported results.

Read the MD&A

You can find a narrative explanation of a company's financial performance in a section of the quarterly or annual report entitled, "Management's Discussion and Analysis of Financial Condition and Results of Operations." **MD&A** *is management's opportunity to provide investors with its view of the financial performance and condition of the company.* It's management's opportunity to tell investors what the financial statements show and do not show, as well as important trends and risks that have shaped the past or are reasonably likely to shape the company's future.

The SEC's rules governing MD&A require disclosure about trends, events, or uncertainties known to management that would have a material impact on reported financial information. The purpose of MD&A is to provide investors with information that the company's management believes to be necessary to an understanding of its financial condition, changes in financial condition, and results of operations. It is intended to help investors to see the company through the eyes of management. It is also intended to provide context for the financial statements and information about the company's earnings and cash flows.

Balance Sheet

A **Balance Sheet** *provides detailed information about a company's assets, liabilities, and shareholders' equity.* A balance sheet shows a snapshot of a company's assets, liabilities, and shareholders' equity at the end of the reporting period. It does not show the flows into and out of the accounts during the period. A balance sheet is a financial statement that summarizes a company's assets, liabilities, and shareholders' equity at a specific point in time. These three balance sheet segments give investors an idea as to what the company owns and owes, as well as the amount invested by the shareholders.

12 Financial Analysis and Time Value of Money

The balance sheet represents a record of a company's assets, liabilities, and equity at a particular point in time. The balance sheet is named by the fact that a business's financial structure balances in the following manner:

$$\text{Assets} = \text{Liabilities} + \text{Shareholders' Equity}$$

Next, you need to know how the balance sheet is set up:

Assets
Current Assets
    Cash
    Accounts Receivable
    Inventories
    Other Current Assets
Total Current Assets
    Property, Plant, Equipment
    Other Assets
Total Assets

Liabilities and Stockholders' Equity
Current Liabilities
    Accounts Payable
    Wages and Other
Expenses Payable
Total Current Liabilities
Long-Term Debt
Other Long-Term Liabilities
Total Liabilities

Stockholders' Equity
Contributed Capital
Retained Earnings
Total Stockholders' Equity
Total Liabilities and Stockholders' Equity

This is an example of a balance sheet. A key item to remember when dealing with a balance sheet: if the Total Assets does not equal Total Liabilities and Stockholder's Equity then you have made a mistake. The balance sheet is named such because of the balance factor.

Assets

So, what exactly are assets? **Assets** *are items you own and do not owe money on*. Assets are anything with commercial value that your business owns. Assets are things that a company owns that have value. This typically means they can either be sold or used by the company to make products or provide services that can be sold. Assets include physical property, such as plants, trucks, equipment, and inventory. It also includes things that can't be touched but nevertheless exist and have value, such as trademarks and patents. And cash itself is an asset. So are investments a company makes. They are divided into three categories: current assets, fixed assets, and other assets. Assets are generally listed based on how quickly they will be converted into cash. Current assets are things a company expects to convert to cash within one year. A good example is an inventory. Most companies expect to sell their inventory for cash within one year. Current assets are cash, accounts receivable, inventory, and other assets that will likely be turned into cash, bartered, exchanged, or converted into an expense within a year during the normal course of business. Included in the "other current assets" category are loans to shareholders, also known as due to shareholders.

The first asset we will discuss is cash. **Cash** *is the money you have in your hand or bank accounts.* Cash is very easy to get to and use. Accounts receivable is the next item we are going to discuss. Accounts receivable is the money that someone owes a company. When customers take out loans to pay off an item, that money is charged to accounts receivable. An inventory is a next item on the balance sheet. Inventories are simply the items you have that you need to sell. Inventories are items that are on your shelf and are constantly changing. All of the items we just discussed are called Total Current Assets when the amounts are totaled together. Current assets are assets that are used within one year.

Long Term Assets *are items like equipment, factories, and property. You do not replace your factories, equipment, and property every year.* When we are talking about the equipment we are not discussing items like office supplies. Equipment would be a printer for a printing company or a mower for a landscaper.

Noncurrent Assets *are things a company does not expect to convert to cash within one year or that would take longer than one year to sell.* Noncurrent assets include fixed assets. Fixed assets are those assets used to operate the business but that are not available for sale, such as trucks, office furniture and other property. Fixed assets have commercial value but are not expected to be consumed or converted into cash in the normal course of business. They are long-term, more permanent or "fixed" items, such as land, building, equipment, fixtures, furniture, and leasehold improvements.

Fixed Assets *often decrease in value (depreciate) over time due to wear and tear from use.* The federal government allows businesses to depreciate items for tax purposes, and it has defined specific depreciation rates for different categories of fixed assets. On your balance sheet, therefore, you will see the initial value of the asset, the amount of accumulated depreciation, and finally the net depreciated value of the asset.

Example of a fixed asset on the balance sheet:

Vehicle	$28,000
Accum Deprec - Vehicle	$-8,500
Total Vehicle	$19,500*

Liabilities

We are going to move to the next section of the balance sheet, the liabilities section. **Liabilities** *are what you owe to other people.* This can include all kinds of obligations, like money borrowed from a bank to launch a new product, rent for use of a building, money owed to suppliers for materials, payroll a company owes to its employees, environmental cleanup costs, or taxes owed to the government. Liabilities also include obligations to provide goods or services to customers in the future. When you take on debt, loans, then you have increased your liabilities. Companies do their best to minimize liabilities. In liabilities, like in assets, there is a section for current liabilities. Current liabilities are going to be accounts payable and wages payable. The term payable means that a company has to pay on that account. Accounts payable is for small or short-term loans, and other bills. Wages payable is the money that needs to be paid to employees. Liabilities are company debts or obligations to outside parties as a result of goods or services that were transferred to your company on a specific date that has already passed. Liabilities are generally listed based on their due dates. Liabilities are said to be either current or long-term. Current liabilities are obligations a company expects to pay off within the year. Long-term liabilities are obligations due more than one year away. Current liabilities are the portion of those obligations that are to be paid out during the year, while long-term liabilities are the portion of your company's obligations that extend beyond that timeframe.

Current Liabilities *include accounts payable, accumulated taxes and payroll liabilities, and the current amount owing on business loans and/or leases.*

16 Financial Analysis and Time Value of Money

Long Term Liabilities *are a company's long-term loans.* These are loans that finance the whole business and will take long periods to pay off. A building loan would be an example of a long-term liability. These liabilities last for more than a year. Long-term liabilities, meanwhile, include the balance of your loans, leases, and other liabilities beyond the current calendar year.

Stockholders' Equity

The next part is Stockholders' equity. Shareholders' equity is sometimes called capital or net worth. **Shareholders' Equity** *is the amount owners invested in the company's stock plus or minus the company's earnings or losses since inception.* Sometimes companies distribute earnings, instead of retaining them. These distributions are called dividends. It's the money that would be left if a company sold all of its assets and paid off all of its liabilities. This leftover money belongs to the shareholders, or the owners, of the company.

A company's assets have to equal, or "balance," the sum of its liabilities and shareholders' equity. Stockholders' equity is money you have gotten from an outside source to help finance a business. Stockholders' equity is very important to a company. Under stockholders' equity, there are two sections: contributed capital and retained earnings. Contributed capital is money that others have contributed to the company. Retained earnings are the money that the company has kept and not paid out to investors. While the company must pay back the investors, a company may re-invest the money to get more money. Once the company has made more money, the company will then pay back the investors.

EXAMPLE: A company's balance sheet is set up like the basic accounting equation shown above. On the left side of the balance sheet, companies list their assets. On the right side, they list their liabilities and shareholders' equity. Sometimes balance sheets show assets at the top, followed by liabilities, with shareholders' equity at the bottom.

Below is an example of a Balance sheet:

Lazy Sofa Furniture Balance Sheet at December 31, 2009 (in Thousands)	
Assets	
Current Assets	
Cash	28
Accounts Receivable	5
Supplies	4
Small Tools	9
Total Current Assets	46
Equipment	18
Other Assets	9
Accumulated Deprecation	(2)
Total Assets	71
Liabilities and Stockholders' Equity	
Current Liabilities	
Accounts Payable	13
Unearned Revenue	3
Wages Payable	3
Interest Payable	1
Income Tax Payable	4

18 Financial Analysis and Time Value of Money

Total Current Liabilities	24
Notes Payable	21
Total Liabilities	45
Stockholders' Equity	
Contributed Capital	20
Retained Earnings	6
Total Stockholders' Equity	26
Total Liabilities ad Stockholders' Equity	71

This example shows you how the assets equal the liabilities and stockholders' equity. The balance sheet is complete and all the information is correct.

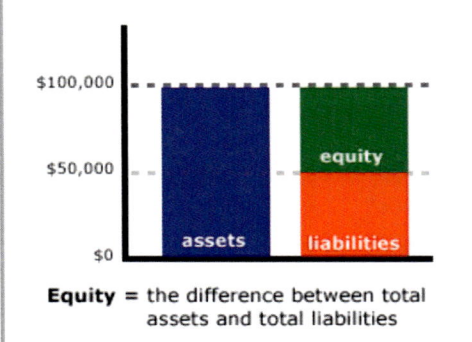

Equity = the difference between total assets and total liabilities

A company's equity is equal to the value of its total assets minus its total liabilities. If the business assets are greater than the liabilities, which is hopefully the case, then the equity of the business is the positive difference between the two numbers.

Stockholder's equity is contributed capital plus retained earnings. Contributed capital is the value of stock that shareholders have directly purchased from the issuing company. When a company issue shares the contributed capital is the initial price of the shares times the number of shares issued. Retained earnings are the amount of money that is retained by the company to be reinvested into the core business or pay off debt. Retained earnings is the percentage of net earnings not paid out as dividends, but retained by the company to be reinvested in its core business or to pay the debt. It is recorded under shareholders' equity on the balance sheet.

The formula calculates retained earnings by adding net income to (or subtracting any net losses from) beginning retained earnings and subtracting any dividends paid to shareholders:

> Retained Earnings (RE) = Beginning RE + Net Income - Dividends

Also known as the "retention ratio" or "retained surplus".

The equity statement explains the changes in retained earnings. Retained earnings appear on the balance sheet and most commonly are influenced by income and dividends. The Statement of Retained Earnings, therefore, uses information from the Income Statement and provides information to the Balance Sheet.

The following equation describes the equity statement for a sole proprietorship:

> Ending Equity = Beginning Equity + Investments - Withdrawals + Income

For a corporation, substitute "Dividends Paid" for "Withdrawals". The stockholders' equity in a corporation is calculated as follows:

```
      Common Stock (recorded at par value)
    + Premium on Common Stock (issue price minus par value)
    + Preferred Stock (recorded at par value)
    + Premium on Preferred Stock (issue price minus par value)
    + Retained Earnings
    ----------------------------------------------------------------
    = Stockholders' Equity
```

Note that the premium on the issuance of stock is based on the price at which the corporation sold the stock on the market. Afterward, market

Income Statement

An **Income Statement** *is a report that shows how much revenue a company earned over a specific period (usually for a year or some portion of a year).* An income statement also shows the costs and expenses associated with earning that revenue. The literal "bottom line" of the statement usually shows the company's net earnings or losses. This tells you how much the company earned or lost over the period. The income statement is different from the balance sheet by the information it tells. An income statement deals with revenues and expenses, while the balance sheet dealing with assets, liabilities, and stockholders' equity. While the balance sheet takes a snapshot approach in examining a business, the income statement measures a company's performance over a specific time frame. Technically, you could have a balance sheet for a month or even a day, but you'll only see public companies report quarterly and annually.

> **Income Statements show how much a company earned or lost over a period of time**

An income statement is a financial statement that measures a company's financial performance over a specific accounting period. Financial performance is assessed by giving a summary of how the business incurs its revenues and expenses through both operating and non-operating activities. It also shows the net profit or loss incurred over a specific accounting period, typically over a fiscal quarter or year.

Also known as the "profit and loss statement" or "statement of revenue and expense".

The income statement presents information about revenues, expenses, and profit that was generated as a result of the business' operations for that period. The reporting of profitability involves two things:

the amount that was earned (revenues) and the expenses necessary to earn the revenues. As you will see next, the

term revenues are not the same as receipts, and the

term expenses involve more than just writing a check to pay a bill. The equation for the income statement is: revenue minus expenses equals net income. Income statements also report earnings per share (or "EPS"). This calculation tells you how much money shareholders would receive if the company decided to distribute all of the net earnings for the period. (Companies seldom distribute all of their earnings. Usually, they reinvest them in the business.)

To understand how income statements are set up, think of them as a set of stairs. You start at the top with the total amount of sales made during the accounting period. Then you go down one step at a time. At each step, you make a deduction for certain costs or other operating expenses associated with earning the revenue. At the bottom of the stairs, after deducting all of the expenses, you learn how much the company earned or lost during the accounting period. People often call this "the bottom line."

At the top of the income statement is the total amount of money brought in from sales of products or services. This top line is often referred to as gross revenues or sales. It's called "gross" because expenses have not been deducted from it yet. So the number is "gross" or unrefined.

The next line is money the company doesn't expect to collect on certain sales. This could be due, for example, to sales discounts or merchandise returns.

When you subtract the returns and allowances from the gross revenues, you arrive at the company's net revenues. It's called "net" because, if you can imagine a net, these revenues are left in the net after the deductions for returns and allowances have come out.

Moving down the stairs from the net revenue line, several lines represent various kinds of operating expenses. Although these lines can be reported in various orders, the next line after net revenues typically shows the costs of the sales. This number tells you the amount of money the company spent to produce the goods or services it sold during the accounting period.

The next line subtracts the costs of sales from the net revenues to arrive at a subtotal called "gross profit" or sometimes "gross margin." It's considered "gross" because there are certain expenses that haven't been deducted from it yet.

The next section deals with operating expenses. These are expenses that go toward supporting a company's operations for a given period – for example, salaries of administrative personnel and costs of researching new products. Marketing expenses are another example. Operating expenses are different from "costs of sales," which were deducted above because operating expenses cannot be linked directly to the production of the products or services being sold. The income statement is spilt into two different sections: operating and non-operating. The operating sections deal with expenses and revenues that are directly tied to the operation of the company. The non-operating section deals with expenses and revenues not directly tied to operating. For example, if a company sells some old equipment, the company gets revenue. However, the revenue from the sale does not have a direct effect on the operation of the company.

Income Statement

Quarterly   Yearly

Revenues
- Net Sales
- Gross Income
- Other

Expenses
- Cost of Sales
- Selling
- General Administrative Expenses
- Other

Net Profit
- Gross Profit
- Operating Profit
- Pretax Profit
- After Tax Profit

Depreciation is also deducted from gross profit. Depreciation takes into account the wear and tear on some assets, such as machinery, tools, and furniture, which are used over the long term. Companies spread the cost of these assets over the periods they are used. This process of spreading these costs is called depreciation or amortization. The "charge" for using these assets during the period is a fraction of the original cost of the assets.

After all, operating expenses are deducted from gross profit; you arrive at operating profit before interest and income tax expenses. This is often called "income from operations." Next, companies must account for interest income and interest expense. Interest income is the money companies make from keeping their cash in interest-bearing savings accounts, money market funds, and the like. On the other hand, interest expense is the money companies paid in interest for money they borrow. Some income statements show interest income and interest expense separately. Some income statements combine the two numbers. The interest income and expense are then added or subtracted from the operating profits to arrive at operating profit before income tax.

Finally, income tax is deducted and you arrive at the bottom line: net profit or net losses. (Net profit is also called net income or net earnings.) This tells you how much the company earned or lost during the accounting period. Did the company make a profit or did it lose money?

The income state is spilt into quarterly and yearly sections. By law publicly traded companies must present their balance sheet and income statement to the public. The reason companies must put out these statements is to ensure the company is functioning properly. Moreover, it is to make sure investors are fully aware of the companies' finances and are not in the dark.

Example:

Lazy Sofa Furniture Income Statement For the Year Ended December 31, 2009	
Revenues	
Service Revenue	$65,000
Total Revenue	$65,000
Expenses	
Operating Expenses	$43,000
Wage Expenses	$3,000
Depreciation Expenses	$2,000
Interest Expenses	$1,000
Income Tax Expenses	$4,000
Total Expenses	$53,000
Net Income	$12,000

In the example, you can see how much the expenses are. The total amount of the expenses is taken from the total revenue. In this example, the statement is set up just a little bit differently. Many of the small amounts are inserted into a broad category. A key thing to remember is:

> Net Income = Revenues − Expenses

Revenues

The first line on any income statement is an entry called total revenue or total sales. This figure is the amount of money a business brought in during the period covered by the income statement. It has nothing to do with profit. If you owned a pizza parlor and sold 10

pizzas for $10 each, you would record $100 of revenue regardless of your profit or loss.

The revenue figure is important because a business must bring in money to turn a profit. If a company has less revenue, all else being equal, it's going to make less money. For startup companies and new ventures that have yet to turn a profit, revenue can sometimes serve as a gauge of potential profitability in the future.

Expenses

The next section of the income statement focuses on the operating expenses that arise during the ordinary course of running a business.

Operating expense consists of salaries paid to employees, research and development costs, legal fees, accountant fees, bank charges, office supplies, electricity bills, business licenses, and more.

The general rule of thumb is that if an expense doesn't qualify as a cost of goods sold, meaning it isn't directly related to producing or manufacturing a good or service, it goes under the operating expense section of the income statement.

Net Income

This is the bottom line, which is the most commonly used indicator of a company's profitability. Of course, if expenses exceed income, this account caption will read as a net loss.

Example:

Income statement for XYZ business for the period ending 31st of December 2010	Budgeted $	Actual $
INCOME		
Services rendered	100,000	94,600
EXPENSES		
Salaries	25,000	25,000
Telephone & internet	6,500	6,500
Water & electricity	14,000	16,000
Property rates and taxes	1,000	1,000
Insurance	7,300	7,300
Advertising costs	1,000	1,000
Fuel	1,800	2,500
Stationery	500	412
Bank charges / interest paid	600	654
Tax expense	3,000	3,414
NET PROFIT	39,300	30,820

Statement of Cash Flows

The **Statement of Cash Flows** represents *a record of a business' cash inflows and outflows over some time*. This is important because a company needs to have enough cash on hand to pay its expenses and purchase assets. While an income statement can tell you whether a company made a profit, a cash flow statement can tell you whether the company generated cash. A cash flow statement shows changes over time rather than absolute dollar amounts at a point in time. It uses and reorders the information from a company's balance sheet and income statement. The bottom line of the cash flow statement shows the net increase or decrease in cash for the period. Generally, cash flow statements are divided into three main parts. Each part reviews the cash flow from one of three types of activities:

1. Operating Activities
2. Investing Activities
3. Financing Activities

Typically, a statement of cash flows focuses on the following cash-related activities:

- **Operating Cash Flow (OCF):** Cash generated from day-to-day business operations
- **Cash from investing (CFI):** Cash used for investing in assets, as well as the proceeds from the sale of other businesses, equipment, or long-term assets
- **Cash from financing (CFF):** Cash paid or received from the issuing and borrowing of funds

Operations

The first part of a cash flow statement analyzes a company's cash flow from net income or losses. For most companies, this section of the cash flow statement reconciles the net income (as shown on the income statement) to the actual cash the company received from or used in its operating activities. To do this, it adjusts net income for any non-cash items (such as adding back depreciation expenses) and adjusts for any cash that was used or provided by other operating assets and liabilities. Cash flow is calculated by making certain adjustments to net income by adding or subtracting differences in revenue, expenses, and credit transactions (appearing on the balance sheet and income statement) resulting from transactions that occur from one period to the next. These adjustments are made because non-cash items are calculated into net income (income statement) and total assets and liabilities (balance sheet). So, because not all transactions involve actual cash items, many items have to be re-evaluated when calculating cash flow from operations.

For example, depreciation is not really a cash expense; it is an amount that is deducted from the total value of an asset that has previously been accounted for. That is why it is added back into net sales for calculating cash flow.

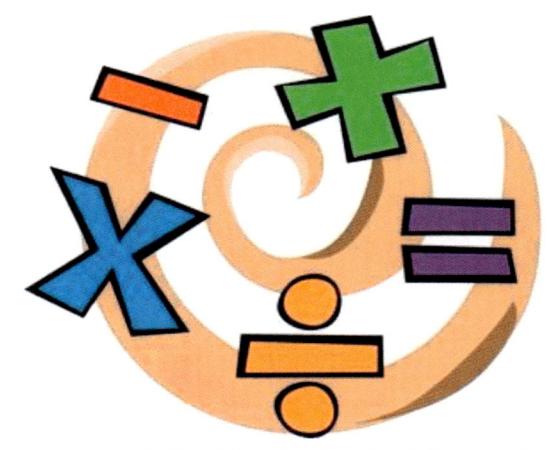

28 Financial Analysis and Time Value of Money

The only time income from an asset is accounted for in CFS calculations is when the asset is sold.

Changes in accounts receivable on the balance sheet from one accounting period to the next must also be reflected in cash flow. If accounts receivable decreases, this implies that more cash has entered the company from customers paying off their credit accounts - the amount by which AR has decreased is then added to net sales. If accounts receivable increase from one accounting period to the next, the amount of the increase must be deducted from net sales because, although the amounts represented in AR are revenue, they are not cash.

An increase in inventory, on the other hand, signals that a company has spent more money to purchase more raw materials. If the inventory was paid with cash, the increase in the value of inventory is deducted from net sales. A decrease in inventory would be added to net sales. If inventory was purchased on credit, an increase in accounts payable would occur on the balance sheet, and the amount of the increase from one year to the other would be added to net sales.

The same logic holds for taxes payable, salaries payable, and prepaid insurance. If something has been paid off, then the difference in the value owed from one year to the next has to be subtracted from net income. If there is an amount that is still owed, then any differences will have to be added to net earnings.

Investing

The second part of a cash flow statement shows the cash flow from all investing activities, which generally include purchases or sales of long-term assets, such as property, plant, and equipment, as well as investment securities. If a company buys a piece of machinery, the cash flow statement would reflect this activity as a cash outflow from investing activities because it used cash. If the company decided to sell off some investments from an investment portfolio, the proceeds from the sales would show up as a cash inflow from investing activities because it provided cash. Changes in equipment, assets, or investments relate to cash from investing. Usually, cash changes from investing are a "cash-out" item, because cash is used to buy new equipment, buildings, or short-term assets such as marketable securities. However, when a company divests an asset, the transaction is considered "cash in" for calculating cash from investing.

Financing

The third part of a cash flow statement shows the cash flow from all financing activities. Typical sources of cash flow include cash raised by selling stocks and bonds or borrowing from banks. Likewise, paying back a bank loan would show up as a use of cash flow. Changes in debt, loans, or dividends are accounted for in cash from financing. Changes in cash from financing are "cash in" when capital is raised, and they're "cash-out" when dividends are paid. Thus, if a company issues a bond to the public, the company receives cash financing; however, when interest is paid to bondholders, the company is reducing its cash.

Example:

Cash Flow Statement Company XYZ FY Ended 31 Dec 2003	
all figures in USD	
Cash Flow From Operations	
Net Earnings	2,000,000
Additions to Cash	
Depreciation	10,000
Decrease in Accounts Receivable	15,000
Increase in Accounts Payable	15,000
Increase in Taxes Payable	2,000
Subtractions From Cash	
Increase in Inventory	(30,000)
Net Cash from Operations	2,012,000
Cash Flow From Investing	
Equipment	(500,000)
Cash Flow From Financing	
Notes Payable	10,000
Cash Flow for FY Ended 31 Dec 2003	1,522,000

Where to Find Financial Statements

Now that you have an understanding of what the three financial statements represent, let's discuss where an investor can go about finding them. In the United States, the Securities And Exchange Commission (SEC) requires all companies that are publicly traded on a major exchange to submit periodic filings detailing their financial activities, including the financial statements mentioned above.

All of this information can be found in the business' annual 10-K and quarterly 10-Q filings, which are released by the company's management and can be found on the internet or in physical form.

The 10-K is an annual filing that discloses a business's performance over the fiscal year. In addition to finding a business's financial statements for the most recent year, investors also have access to the business's historical financial measures, along with

Financial Analysis and Time Value of Money 31

information detailing the operations of the business. This includes a lot of information, such as the number of employees, biographies of upper management, risks, plans for growth, etc.

Businesses also release an annual report, which some people also refer to as the 10-K. The annual report is essentially the 10-K released in a fancier marketing format. It will include much of the same information, but not all, that you can find in the 10-K. The 10-K really is boring - it's just pages and pages of numbers, text, and legalese. But just because it's boring doesn't mean it isn't useful. There is a lot of good information in a 10-K, and it's required reading for any serious investor.

You can think of the 10-Q filing as a smaller version of a 10-K. It reports the company's performance after each fiscal quarter. Each year three 10-Q filings are released - one for each of the first three quarters. (Note: There is no 10-Q for the fourth quarter because the 10-K filing is released during that time). Unlike the 10-K filing, 10-Q filings are not required to be audited. Here's a tip if you have trouble remembering which is which: think "Q" for the quarter.

All of the 10-ks and 10-qs can be found at *www.sec.gov*. Mush of the same information can be found on different financial websites such as *www.finance.yahoo.com* or *www.morningstar.com*.

ACTIVITY

Spend time looking up different companies that are of interest to you and look at their financial statements.

2: Financial Ratios

you could have been introduced in a previous book by the same author (check the Foundations of Risk and Return book, by Dr. Juan R. Castro) about the idea of risk and return on investment. "High risk, high returns. Low risk, low return." is the saying that you will hear often in the financial world. It is the truth. However financial professions also develop many different techniques and instruments to help you minimizing the risk and assuring return on your investment. Financial ratios analysis is one of those methods available to help you make better decisions. Most people get nervous about the term. Don't be!!! They may sound complicated, but once you get to know them, they are actually very simple concepts. Financial ratios are very useful tools for analyzing the financial strength of a company, but for a financial ratio to have any significance it must be compared to a benchmark of some kind. The benchmark can be several things like the best performing company in that industry, an industry average, or previous periods of the company you are analyzing. The purpose of this tutorial is to provide you with a guide to expose and define the most relevant ratios, to show you how to calculate them, what their significance is, and to explain their meaning to you as an investor.

Financial ratios analysis is a technique that uses a time-tested method to measure a business's health. Wall Street investment firms, bank loan officers, and knowledgeable business owners all use financial ratio analysis to learn more about a company's current situation as well as to forecast its potential in the future. Although they may be somewhat unfamiliar concepts to you, I guarantee financial ratios are neither sophisticated nor complicated. As you can recall from school, the ratio is the

Financial Analysis and Time Value of Money 33

relationship between two numbers. As your high school math teacher might have put it as "the relative size of two quantities, expressed as of one divided by the other." It is nothing, but simple comparisons between specific pieces of information already available in the company's balance sheet and income statement.

Financial ratio analysis is essential for investment in two ways. First, you can use them to examine the current performance of your company in comparison to past periods, from the prior quarters to years ago. Essentially, this helps you to identify operating problems that need to be fixed if you are one of the executives. Even better, as investors, it can direct your attention to potential problems that can be avoided. Evidence suggests that as early as five years before a firm fails, one may be able to detect trouble from the value of these financial ratios. Secondly, you can use these ratios to compare the performance of your company against that of your competitors or other members within a specific industry. Nowadays, most financial websites like Google Finance or Yahoo Finance often provide you the most information about the company including their calculated ratios. Therefore, in this module, we will just briefly cover the calculation. The majority part will rather focus on the meaning of the ratio and how it can be useful for your investment decisions.

You've probably heard people banter around phrases like "P/E ratio," "current ratio" and "operating margin." But what do these terms mean and why don't they show up on financial statements? Listed below are just some of the many ratios that investors calculate from information on financial statements and then use to evaluate a company. As a general rule, desirable ratios vary by industry.

Earnings per Share (EPS) or E/S

Most income statements include a calculation of earnings per share or EPS. This calculation tells you how much money shareholders would receive for each share of stock they own if the company distributed all of its net income for the period.

To calculate EPS, you take the total net income and divide it by the number of outstanding shares of the company. The EPS is one of the most widely reported ratios and is included here because it can be used to help find other ratios that can compare a company to other companies and industry standards. EPS takes the net profit after tax and subtracts it from the number of dividends paid out to shareholders, all divided by the number of outstanding shares. The formula is below:

$$EPS = \frac{Net\ profit\ after\ taxes - Preferred\ Dividends}{Number\ of\ common\ shares\ outstanding}$$

EXAMPLE

A company has $1,500,000 profit after taxes and pays out $150,000 worth of dividends. There are 200,000 outstanding shares.

$$EPS = \frac{\$1,500,000 - \$150,000}{200,000} = \$6.75/share$$

Price Earnings Ratio (P/E)

(P/E) is one of the best known valuation indicators. The financial reporting of both companies and investment research services use a basic earnings per share (EPS) figure divided into the current stock price to calculate the P/E ratio. Analyst estimates based on forward-looking projections of a company's earnings have a significant effect of how a stock is valued on

Wall Street. It is important to note, that while a company may have sound financial ratios and a good P/E ratio, its stock price can still fall if it doesn't meet the expectations of Wall Street analysts. Historically, the average P/E ratio for the general market has been around 15. This is not a hard and true number to go by as economic conditions can significantly affect the financial stability of companies. The ratio will also vary widely among different companies and industries. This is an extension of the EPS and it relates the earnings to the price of the stock as follows:

$$P/E = \frac{Market\ price\ of\ common\ stock}{EPS}$$

This particular ratio is good for telling you how much investors are willing to pay for a stock relative to the company's earnings. This ratio lets you know how many dollars you are paying for one dollar of earnings. This ratio is great for comparing companies in the same ratio so you can see who is best at turning your money into profit. The basic formula for calculating the P/E ratio is easy to calculate and the information necessary to do the calculation is easy to find on most any finance website. A stock with a high P/E ratio suggests that investors are expecting higher earnings growth in the future compared to the overall market because investors are paying more for today's earnings in anticipation of future earnings growth. Stocks that have a higher P/E ratio than the market average are considered to be growth stocks. Conversely, a stock with a low P/E ratio suggests that investors have more modest expectations for its future growth compared to the market as a whole. If a company's stock is selling at $20 per share and the company is earning $2 per share, then the company's P/E Ratio is 10 to 1. The company's stock is selling at 10 times its earnings.

Price to Sales Ratio (PSR)

The PSR relates sales per share to the market price of the company's stock. This measure is often used to identify overpriced stocks - stocks that should be avoided. The principle is that the lower the PSR the less likely it is that the stock will be overpriced. PSR is computed as follows:

$$PSR = \frac{Market\ price\ of\ common\ stock}{Annual\ sales\ per\ share}$$

$$PSR = \frac{38}{9.54} = 3.98$$

In the case of EMC, the PSR is 3.98, or an indication that the market price of the stock is four times the annual sales per share.

Annual Sales per Share

This is a ratio used in the computation of the PSR (above) and is computed as follows:

$$Annual\ Sales/share = \frac{Annual\ revenue}{Number\ of\ common\ shares\ outstanding}$$

Shows a company's business activities versus the share price. The higher the ratio, the more active the company is.

Dividend per Share

This is the dividend equivalent to EPS and is determined by dividing the annual dividend by the number of common shares outstanding. This shows you how much a company will pay you out per stock you own.

Payout Ratio

This is the ratio between dividends and earnings per share. The computation is as follows:

$$Payout\ ratio = \frac{Dividends\ per\ share}{EPS}$$

This ratio lets you see what a company is doing with its earnings. Also, the lower the ratio, the more secure the dividend is because smaller payout ratios are easier to maintain.

Book Value per Share

A measure of stockholder's equity. It shows how much each share is worth after all of a company's debts are paid off. It is a measure of safety for the shareholder. It represents the difference between total assets and total liabilities. It is computed as follows:

$$Book\ value\ per\ share = \frac{Stockholders'\ equity}{Number\ of\ common\ share\ outstanding}$$

Price to Book Ratio

This is a convenient way to relate the book value of a company to the market price of its stock. It is computed as follows:

$$Price-to-book\ value = \frac{Market\ price\ of\ common\ stock}{Book\ value\ per\ share}$$

$$EMC = \frac{38}{6.87} = 5.53$$

Widely used to indicate how aggressively the stock is being priced. We would expect the value to be over 1 which would indicate that the market price is = to the book value. In a bull market, this Price to Book Value may reach multiples of 2, 3, or higher.

Net Profit Margin

This is the "bottom line" of operations. It indicates the rate of profit from sales and other revenues. The net profit margin is computed as follows:

$$Net\ profit\ margin = \frac{Net\ profit\ after\ taxes}{Total\ revenue}$$

$$MC = \frac{386{,}229}{2{,}273{,}652} = .17$$

In the example above, we see that for every dollar made, the company keeps $.17 as profit. Net Profit Margin is a measure of profitability. If the margin were negative, it would mean the company was losing money on its sales.

Operating Margin

Compares a company's operating income to net revenues. Both of these numbers can be found on a company's income statement. To calculate operating margin, you divide a company's income from operations (before interest and income tax expenses) by its net revenues, or

$$Operating\ margin = \frac{Income\ from\ operations}{Net\ revenues}$$

The operating margin is usually expressed as a percentage. It shows, for each dollar of sales, what percentage was profit.

Personal Finance Ratios

These are ratios you need to know to make sure that your household finances are in order.

Savings Ratio

Should be between 10% to 20%. The ratio of current period's cash surplus to the current period's income after taxes. If a household wanted to put 15% of their income into their savings account, this is the ratio they would use. Assuming they make $48,000 a year.

$48,000/ 12 months = $4,000/ month $4,000 (.15) = $600/ month to put into savings.

You can make this apply to your situation by changing the income to match yours, and the percent to the percent you want to set aside monthly.

Debt-to-Income Ratio (DTI)

Debt-to-equity ratio compares a company's total debt to shareholders' equity. Both of these numbers can be found on a company's balance sheet. Finds out how what percentage of a household's income goes towards paying debts. The formula takes into account monthly reoccurring debts (taxes, insurance, mortgage, loans, and insurance) and divides it by your household's monthly income. The formula is important for qualifying for loans on a house or car. Banks want you to keep the ratio below 36% as it shows that you can maintain your debts and income.

$$DTI\ Ratio = \frac{Monthly\ reoccurring\ detbs}{Monthly\ income}$$

EXAMPLE

Yearly Gross Income = $45,000 / Divided by 12 = $3,750 per month income.

$3,750 Monthly Income x .36 = $1,350 allowed for housing expense plus recurring debt.

If a company has a debt-to-equity ratio of 2 to 1, it means that the company has two dollars of debt to every one dollar shareholders invest in the company. In other words, the company is taking on debt at twice the rate that its owners are investing in the company.

Housing Cost Ratio

Should not exceed 28% of gross income. Total of monthly mortgage payment (principal + interest), plus 1/12th of annual real estate taxes, plus 1/12th of the annual homeowner's insurance premium, plus 1/12th of the annual association fees divided by the gross (before tax) monthly income.

EXAMPLE

Yearly Gross Income = $45,000 / Divided by 12 = $3,750 per month income.

$3,750 Monthly Income x .28 = $1,050 allowed for housing expense.

Consumer Debt Ratio

Should not exceed 20%. This is the ratio of monthly consumer debt payments to monthly (after-tax) income. Add credit card payments, auto loan payments, and department store account payments.

Total Debt Ratio

The debt ratio compares a company's total debt to its total assets, which is used to gain a general idea as to the amount of borrowed money being used by a company. A low percentage means that the company is less dependent on money borrowed from and owed to others. The lower the percentage, the less leverage a company is using and the stronger its equity position. In general, the higher the ratio, the more risk that company is considered to have taken on, and conversely the lower the ratio the less risk this company is taking.

Formula:

$$\text{Debt Ratio} = \frac{\text{Total liabilities}}{\text{Total assets}}$$

The debt ratio is simple to calculate and is very helpful to investors looking for a snap shot of how much money a company has borrowed compared to its total amount of assets. The more debt compared to assets a company the riskier the company is considered to be. A high debt ratio signals that the company may have too much debt on its balance sheets. Should not exceed 36% of gross income. Calculated by dividing total monthly loan payments by the gross (before taxes) monthly income.

Working Capital

The money leftover if a company paid its current liabilities (that is, its debts due within one-year of the date of the balance sheet) from its current assets.

> Working Capital = Current Assets – Current Liabilities

These ratios are just a few examples of fundamental analysis that is used to evaluate a company's investment quality. It is very important to consider several factors when looking at financial ratios. Financial ratios are very useful in identifying trends within a company and within an industry, which is why it is important to always compare financial ratios to benchmark figures with a specific sector of the market.

Liquidity Ratios

To survive, firms must be able to meet their short-term obligations of paying their creditors and their short-term debts - liquidity. Thus, the liquidity of the firm can be measure as a firm's financial health. Two common formulas measuring liquidity are:

42 Financial Analysis and Time Value of Money

> Current ratio = current assets / current liabilities

> Quick ratio = (cash + marketable securities + net receivables) / current liabilities

Current Ratio

To begin, the current ratio is a commonly used ratio to test a company's liquidity by finding the number of current assets available to cover current liabilities. The concept behind this ratio is to find out whether a company's short-term assets which are cash, cash equivalents, marketable securities, receivables, and inventory that are readily available to pay off its short-term liabilities; which are: notes payable, current term debt, payables, accrued expenses and taxes. The significance of the current ratio is that the higher the current ratio the better the company is equipped to pay off its short-term debt. A ratio under 1 means that a person could not pay their debtors if they had to pay them back at the present moment. Ideally, a person would have a ratio greater than 1 because they would have more assets than liabilities and therefore could pay off any liabilities.

Quick Ratio

The quick ratio is also known as the quick assets ratio is another liquidity ratio that narrows down the focus of the current ratio by measuring the amount of the most liquid current assets there are to cover current liabilities. The quick ratio is more precise in its definition of current assets than the current ratio because it excludes inventory and other current assets, which are more difficult to turn into cash. A higher ratio means a more liquid current position, which is typically better for a company. All of the information that is needed to calculate the quick ratio can be found on the balance sheet. The balance sheet gives a good overall picture of the long-term structure of the company's financials and this information is very useful. But, there are areas that the balance sheet does not cover in the data that it presents. The income statement, however, gives a better representation of a company's normal operating costs. In the income statement, there are two areas of profit margins that we will focus on. Keep in mind that there are several other areas of profit that the income statement shows as well. For this section, we will focus on gross profit and net profit. Profit margin analysis uses the percentage calculation to provide a comprehensive measure of a company's profitability on a historical basis generally looking at the 3-5-year time period and in comparison to similar companies and industry benchmarks. The objective of margin analysis is to detect consistency and trends in a company's earnings. Positive profit margin analysis usually translates into positive investment quality. Profits, or earnings, are what drives the stock price of a company, so a company that has consistently increased earnings will usually have a consistently increasing stock price. Also, if a company has stagnant or decreasing earnings then their stock price will most likely be stagnant or declining as well.

The main difference between the current ratio and the quick ratio is that the latter does not include inventories, while the former does. In some ways, the quick ratio is a more conservative standard. If the quick ratio is greater than one, there would seem to be no danger that the firm would not be able to meet its current obligations. If the quick ratio is less than one, but the current ratio is considerably above one, the status of the firm is more complex. In this case, the valuation of inventories and the inventory turnover are obviously critical.

> **The main difference between current and quick ratios: current ratios include inventories and quick ratios do not**

The inventory turnover ratio compares a company's cost of sales on its income statement with its average inventory balance for the period. To calculate the average inventory balance for the period, look at the inventory numbers listed on the balance sheet. Take the balance listed for the period of the report and add it to the balance listed for the previous comparable period, and then divide by two. (Remember that balance sheets are snapshots in time. So the inventory balance for the previous period is the beginning balance for the current period, and the inventory balance for the current period is the ending balance.) To calculate the inventory turnover ratio, you divide a company's cost of sales (just below the net revenues on the income statement) by the average inventory for the period, or:

$$Inventory\ turnover\ ratio = \frac{Cost\ of\ sales}{Average\ inventory\ for\ the\ period}$$

If a company has an inventory turnover ratio of 2 to 1, it means that the company's inventory turned over twice in the reporting period.

Though helpful, current ratios can inaccurately measure a firm's performance in several circumstances. First of all various accounting methods used by different companies often create problems. For example, there are two methods of counting inventories: FIFO (First In First Out) and LIFO (Last In First Out). Under the LIFO method, inventories are valued at their old costs. Under the FIFO method of inventory valuation, inventories are valued at close to their current replacement cost. Therefore, inventory may be undervalued or overvalued according to market movement. Clearly, if we have firms that differ in their accounting methods, and hold substantial inventories, comparisons of current ratios will not be very helpful in measuring their relative strength, unless accounting differences are adjusted for in the computations. A second problem with including inventories in the current ratio derives from the difference between the inventory's accounting value, however calculated, and its economic value. A simple example is a firm subject to business-cycle fluctuations. For a firm of this sort, inventories will typically build during a downturn. The posted market price for the inventoried product will often not fall very much during this period; nevertheless, the firm finds it cannot sell very much of its inventoried product at the so-called market price.

The growing inventory is carried at the posted price, but there really is no way that the firm could liquidate that inventory to meet current obligations. Thus, including inventories in current assets will tend to understate the precarious financial position of firms suffering inventory buildup during downturns. However, we can't conclude that the quick ratio is always to be preferred. If we ignore inventories, firms with readily marketable inventories, appropriately valued, will be undeservedly penalized. Clearly, some judicious further investigation of the marketability of the inventories would be helpful.

Low values for the current or quick ratios suggest that a firm may have difficulty meeting current obligations. Low values, however, are not always a bad thing. If an organization has good long-term prospects, it may be able to enter the capital market and borrow against those prospects to meet current obligations. The nature of the business itself might also allow it to operate with a current ratio of less than one. For example, in an operation like McDonald's, inventory turns over much more rapidly than the accounts payable become due. This timing difference can also allow a firm to operate with a low current ratio. Finally, to the extent that the current and quick ratios are helpful indexes of a firm's financial health, they act strictly as signals of trouble at extreme rates. Some liquidity is useful for an organization, but a very high current ratio might suggest that the firm is sitting around with a lot of cash because it lacks the managerial acumen to put those resources to work. Very low liquidity, on the other hand, is also problematic.

These ratios are important to know if you plan to invest in the stock market. These financial ratios are key to understanding a company's financial reports.

Gross Profit Margin

A company's cost of sales, or **Cost of Goods Sold**, *represents the expense related to labor, raw materials, and manufacturing overhead involved in its production process*. This expense is deducted from the company's net sales/revenue, which results in a company's first level of profit, or gross profit. The gross profit margin is used to analyze how efficiently a company is using its raw materials, labor, and manufacturing-related assets to generate profits. The higher the margin percentage means that the company is efficiently using its resources to generate a profit. To obtain the gross profit amount, simply subtract the cost of goods sold from net sales also known as net revenues. The operating profit amount is found by subtracting the sum of the company's operating expenses from the gross profit amount. Generally, operating expenses would include accounts titled as selling, marketing and administrative, research and development, depreciation, and amortization. This can all be found in the income statements of the company.

$$Gross\ profit\ margin = \frac{Gross\ profit}{Net\ sales\ (revenue)}$$

When these ratios are measured over time they show the trend of management's ability to manage costs and expenses and generate profits.

The successes or failures of the management's ability to generate profits are what determine a company's profitability.

Net Profit Margin

Often referred to simply as a company's profit margin, or the bottom line is the most often mentioned when discussing a company's profitability. This is a significant ratio because it is directly related to how much money the company is making from its goods or services. It is calculated by dividing the net income by the net sales.

$$Net\ profit\ margin = \frac{Net\ income}{Net\ sales\ (revenue)}$$

It is extremely important for anyone who is investing to take a comprehensive look at a company's profit margins over an extended timeline to understand the direction the company is heading. Another important note about profitability ratios is that they must be compared to benchmarks within the industry to understand what "good" levels of profitability are.

Leverage

Firms are often financed by a combination of debt and equity. The right capital structure will depend on tax policy—high corporate rates favor debt, high personal tax rates favor equity—on bankruptcy costs, and overall corporate risk. There are two commonly used measures of leverage, the debt-to-assets ratio, and the debt-equity ratio:

$$Debt-to-asset\ ratio = \frac{Total\ liabilities}{Total\ assets}$$

$$\text{Debt-to-equity ratio} = \frac{\text{Long-term debt}}{\text{Shareholders' equity}}$$

As with liquidity measures, problems in measurement and interpretation also occur in leverage measures. The central problem is that assets and equity are typically measured in terms of the carrying (book) value in the firm's financial statements. This figure, however, often has very little to do with the market value of the firm, or the value that creditors could receive was the firm liquidated.

Debt-to-equity ratios vary considerably across industries, in large measure due to other characteristics of the industry and its environment. A utility, for example, which is a stable business, can comfortably operate with a relatively high debt-equity ratio. A more cyclical business, like the manufacturing of recreational vehicles, typically needs a lower D/E—a reminder that cross-industry comparisons of these ratios is typically not very helpful.

Often, analysts look at the debt-equity ratio to determine the ability of an organization to generate new funds from the capital market. An organization with considerable debt is often thought to have little new financing capacity. Of course, the overall financing capacity of an organization probably has as much to do with the quality of the new product the organization wishes to pursue as with its financial structure. Nevertheless, given the threat of bankruptcy and the attendant costs, a very high debt-equity ratio may make future financing difficult. It has been argued, for example, that railroads in the 1970s found it hard to find funds for new investments in piggybacking, a large technical improvement in railroading because the threat of bankruptcy from prior poor investments was so high.

Rates of Return

There are two measures of profitability common in the financial community, return on assets (ROA) and return on equity (ROE).

$$ROA = \frac{Net\ income}{Total\ average\ assets}$$

$$ROE = \frac{Net\ income}{Total\ stockholders'equity}$$

Return on Assets: *This ratio indicates how profitable a company is relative to the total amount of assets they hold.* The return on assets (ROA) ratio shows how well management is employing the company's total assets to make a profit. Similar to profit margin analysis, ROA, illustrates how efficiently the company uses all of its assets. The higher the return, the more efficient management is in using the assets of the company. The ROA ratio is calculated by comparing net income to average total assets and is expressed as a percentage. Once again it is extremely important to look at several other companies that operate in the same sector to gauge if the ROA of a single company is significant in its respective industry.

Return on Equity: *This ratio indicates how profitable a company is by comparing its net income to its average shareholders' equity.* The return on equity (ROE) measures how much the shareholders earned for their investment in the company. The higher the ratio percentage, the more efficient management is in utilizing its equity base and the better return is to investors. This is obviously an important ratio for investors to look at because it directly relates to the value that the management of the company will create for its shareholders. The ROE ratio is an important measure of a company's earnings performance. The ROE tells common shareholders how effectively their money is being employed.

Assets and equity, as used in these two common indexes, are both measured in terms of book value. Thus, if assets were acquired some time ago at a low price, the current performance of the organization may be overstated by the use of historically valued denominators. As a result, the accounting returns for any investment generally do not correlate well with the true economic internal rate of return for that investment.

Difficulties with using either ROA and ROE as a performance measure can be seen in merger transactions. Suppose we have an organization that has been earning a net income of $500 on assets with a book value of $1000, for a hefty ROA of 50 percent. That organization is now acquired by a second firm, which then moves the new assets onto its books at the acquisition price, assuming the acquisition is treated using the purchase method of accounting. Of course, the acquisition price will be considerably above the $1,000 book value of assets, for the potential acquirer will have to pay handsomely for the privilege of earning $500 regularly. Suppose the acquirer pays $2,000 for the assets. After the acquisition, it will appear that the returns of the acquired firm have fallen. The firm continues to earn $500, but the asset base is now $2,000, so the ROA is reduced to 25 percent. Indeed, the ROA may be less as a result of other factors, such as increased depreciation of the newly acquired assets. Yet nothing has happened to the earnings of the firm. All that has changed is its accounting, not its performance.

Another fundamental problem with ROA and ROE measures comes

from the tendency of analysts to focus on performance in single years, years that may be idiosyncratic. At a minimum, one should examine these ratios averaging over several years to isolate idiosyncratic returns and try to find patterns in the data.

Evaluations and Exams for Financial Decision Courses

One way is through Cost-Benefit Analysis. This is a process by which business decisions are analyzed. The benefits of a given situation or business-related action are summed and then the costs associated with taking that action are subtracted. Some consultants or analysts also build the model to put a dollar value on intangible items, such as the benefits and costs associated with living in a certain town. Most analysts will also factor opportunity cost into such equations.

Cost-Benefit Analysis deals a lot with Opportunity costs. Those are the following:

1. The cost of an alternative must be forgone to pursue a certain action. Put another way, the benefits you could have received by taking an alternative action.
2. The difference in return between a chosen investment and one that is necessarily passed up. Say you invest in a stock and it returns a paltry 2% over the year. In placing your money in the stock, you gave up the opportunity of another investment - say, a risk-free government bond yielding 6%. In this situation, your opportunity costs are 4% (6% - 2%).

The opportunity cost of going to college is the money you would have earned if you worked instead. On the one hand, you lose four years of salary while getting your degree; on the other hand, you hope to earn more during your career, thanks to your education, to offset the lost wages.

Here's another example: if a gardener decides to grow carrots, his or her opportunity cost is the alternative crop that might have been grown instead (potatoes, tomatoes, pumpkins, etc.).

In both cases, a choice between two options must be made. It would be an easy decision if you knew the end outcome; however, the risk that you could achieve greater "benefits" (be they monetary or otherwise) with another option is the opportunity cost.

http://www.investopedia.com/video/play/opportunity-cost

Opportunity costs can also be divided into a section called cost of acquisition. That is a business sales term referring to the expense required to attain a customer or a sale. In setting a marketing and sales strategy, a company must decide what the maximum cost of acquisition will be, which effectively determines the highest amount the company is willing to spend to attain each customer.

EXAMPLE: Cost-Benefit Analysis

As the Production Manager, you are proposing the purchase of a $1 Million stamping machine to increase output. Before you can present the proposal to the Vice President, you know you need some facts to support your suggestion, so you decide to run the numbers and do a cost-benefit analysis.

You itemize the benefits. With the new machine, you can produce 100 more units per hour. The three workers currently doing the stamping by hand can be replaced. The units will be higher quality because they will be more uniform. You are convinced these outweigh the costs.

There is a cost to purchase the machine and it will consume some electricity. Any other costs would be insignificant.

You calculate the selling price of the 100 additional units per hour multiplied by the number of production hours per month. Add to that two percent for the units that aren't rejected because of the quality of the machine output. You also add the monthly salaries of the three workers. That's a pretty good total benefit.

Then you calculate the monthly cost of the machine, by dividing the purchase price by 12 months per year and divide that by the 10 years the machine should last. The manufacturer's specs tell you what the power consumption of the machine is and you can get power cost numbers from accounting so you figure the cost of electricity to run the machine and add the purchase cost to get a total cost figure.

You subtract your total cost figure from your total benefit value and your analysis shows a healthy profit. All you have to do now is present it to the VP, right? Wrong. You've got the right idea, but you left out a lot of detail.

Accurate Cost-Benefit Analysis

Once you have collected ALL the positive and negative factors and have quantified them you can put them together into an accurate cost-benefit analysis.

Some people like to total up all the positive factors (benefits), total up all the negative factors (costs), and find the difference between the two. I prefer to group the factors. It makes it easier for you, and anyone reviewing your work, to see that you have included all the factors on both sides of the issues that make up the cost-benefit analysis. For the example above, our cost-benefit analysis might look something like this:

Cost Benefit Analysis - Purchase of New Stamping Machine
(Costs shown are per month and amortized over four years)

Purchase of Machine .... -$20,000
includes interest and taxes

Installation of Machine .... -3,125
including screens & removal of existing stampers

Increased Revenue 27,520
net value of additional 100 units per hour, 1 shift/day, 5 days/week

Quality Increase Revenue 358
calculated at 75% of current reject rate

Reduced material costs 1,128
purchase of bulk supply reduces cost by $0.82 per hundred

Reduced Labor Costs 18,585
3 operators salary plus labor o/h

New Operator .... -8,321
salary plus overhead. Includes training

Utilities .... -250
power consumption increase for new machine

Insurance .... -180
premiums increase

Square footage 0
no additional floor space is required

Net Savings per Month $15,715

Your cost benefit analysis clearly shows the purchase of the stamping machine is justified. The machine will save your company over $15,000 per month, almost $190,000 a year.

This is just one example of how you can use cost benefit analysis determine the advisability of a course of action and then to support it once you propose the action.

Financial Analysis and Time Value of Money

Application:

Marriott International, Inc. is a worldwide operator and franchisor of hotels and related lodging facilities. The Company has five business segments: North American Full-Service Lodging, North American Limited-Service Lodging, International Lodging, Luxury Lodging, and Timeshare. It develops, operates, and franchises hotels and corporate housing properties under separate brand names, and it develops, operates, and markets timeshare, fractional ownership, and residential properties under four separate brand names. The Company also provides services to home/condominium owner associations for projects associated with one of its brands.

("Profile: Marriott International, Inc. (MAR)" Full Description)

MARRIOTT INTERNATIONAL, INC. is currently the leader of the lodging industry with more than 3,400 lodging properties in 70 countries and territories. The company is headquartered in Bethesda, Maryland, USA, and had approximately 137,000 employees at 2009 year-end. It is recognized by FORTUNE® as one of the best companies to work for, and by Newsweek as one of the greenest big companies in America. In the fiscal year 2009, Marriott International reported sales from continuing operations of nearly $11 billion. ("Marriott International Company Profile")

ACTIVITY

Perform finance analysis for MARRIOTT INTERNATIONAL, INC. with information from *http://finance.yahoo.com/q?s=MAR&ql=1*.

Ratios applied to Marriott International Inc. and Evaluation (notice that these values may change depending on the year or quarter you are using):

1. Liquidity Ratios

Quick Ratio

Quick Ratio (As of 2007-12-28) = (Current assets – Inventory)/ Current Liabilities

$$= (3{,}572 - 1{,}557) / 2{,}876$$
$$= 0.700$$

Quick Ratio (As of 2010-01-01) = (Current Assets − Inventory)/ Current Liabilities
$$= (2{,}851 - 1{,}444) / 2{,}287$$
$$= 0.615$$

⇨ Marriott International Inc.'s Quick Ratio as of December 28, 2007, is higher than its Quick Ratio as of January 1, 2010. That means the firm's ability to pay off its current debts is decreased over this period.

⇨ The liquidity position is weaker.

2. Assets Management Ratios
Days Sales Outstanding (DSO)

DSO (As of 2007-12-28) = Receivables/ Average Sales per Days
$$= 1{,}148 / (12{,}990 / 365)$$
$$= 32 \text{ days}$$

DSO (As of 2010-01-01) = Receivables/ Average Sales per Days
$$= 838 / (10{,}908 / 365)$$
$$= 28 \text{ days}$$

⇨ Days Sales Outstanding on 2010-01-01 is 4 days less than Days Sales Outstanding on 2007-12-28 which means the company has improved its ability to collect debts from customers.

3. Total Assets Turnover Ratio

Total Assets Turnover Ratio (2007-12-28) = Sales / Total assets
$$= 12{,}990 / 8{,}942$$
$$= 1.45$$

Total Assets Turnover Ratio (2010-01-01) = Sales / Total assets
$$= 10{,}908 / 7{,}933$$
$$= 1.37$$

⇨ Total assets turnover in 2009 is lower than total assets turnover in 2007 shows that the firm does not generate profit as sufficient as it used to do.

4. Debt Management Ratio

Debt ratio (2007-12-28) = Total liabilities / Total assets
$$= 7{,}513 / 8{,}942$$
$$= 0.84$$

Debt ratio (2010-01-01) = Total liabilities / Total Assets
$$= 6{,}791 / 7{,}993$$

= 0.85
⇨ The debt ratio has not changed much from 2007 to 2010. The numbers show that creditors supply money for most of the firm's assets.

5. *Profitability Ratio*
Net Profit Margin (2007- 12- 28) = Net Income / Sales
= 696 / 12,990
= 0.053 = 5.3%
Net Profit Margin (2010- 01- 01) = Net Income / Sales
= -346 / 10,908
= -0.032 = -3.2%
⇨ Net Profit Margin of 2010 is decreased significantly from 5.3% to -3.2% due to a big unusual expense.

6. *Market Value Ratios*
Price/Earnings Ratio = Price per share / Earnings per Share
(2007- 12- 28) = 33.33 / (696/361.1)
= 17.29

Price/Earnings Ratio = Price per share / Earning per Share
(2010- 01- 01) = 27.15 / (-346 / 358.2)
= -28.11

⇨ In 2010, Price/ Earnings Ratio become negative which indicates that the firm is either becoming riskier or having a poorer growth prospect.

ACTIVITY

Pick one company you want to invest in and perform financial analysis. Discuss.

3: Time Value of Money

Let's first learn some definitions used in Time Value of Money

- **Future Value (FV),** *the value of a present amount at a future date, is calculated by applying compound interest over a specific period.* **Present value (PV)** *represents the dollar value today of a future amount, or the amount you would invest today at a given interest rate for a specified period to equal the future amount. Financial managers prefer present value to future value because they typically make decisions at time zero, before the start of a project. A* **Single Amount** *of cash flow refers to an individual standalone value occurring at one point in time. An* **Annuity** *consists of an unbroken series of cash flows of equal dollar amount occurring over more than one period. A* **Mixed Stream** *is a pattern of cash flows over more than one time period, and the amount of cash associated with each period will vary.*
- **Compounding of Interest** *occurs when an amount is deposited into a savings account and the interest paid after the specified period remains in the account, thereby becoming part of the principal for the following period.* The general equation for future value in year n (FV_n) can be expressed using the specified notation as follows:

$$FV_n = PV(1 + r)^n$$

A decrease in the interest rate lowers the future amount of a deposit for a given holding period because the deposit earns less at the lower rate. An increase in the holding period for a given interest rate would increase the future value. The increased holding period increases the *FV* because the deposit earns interest over a longer period.

- Present value is the current dollar value of a future amount. It indicates how much money today would be equivalent to the future amount if one could invest that amount at a specified rate of interest. Using the given notation, the present value of a future amount (FV_n) can be defined as follows:

$$PV = FV_n \div (1 + r)^n$$

An increasing required rate of return would reduce the present value of a future amount because future dollars would be worthless today. Looking at the formula for present value, it should be clear that by increasing the *i* value, which is the required return, the present value of the future sum would decrease.

Present value calculations are the exact inverse of compound interest calculations. Using compound interest, one attempts to find the future value of a present amount; using discounting, one attempts to find the present value of an amount to be received in the future.

- An **Ordinary Annuity** *is one for which payments occur at the end of each period.* An **Annuity Due** *is one for which payments occur at the beginning of each period.*

The ordinary annuity is the more common. For otherwise identical annuities and interest rates, the annuity due results in a higher FV because cash flows occur earlier and have more time to compound. The most efficient ways to calculate the present value of an ordinary annuity are using an algebraic equation, a financial calculator, or a spreadsheet program. You can calculate the future value of an annuity due by multiplying the value calculated for an ordinary annuity by one plus the interest rate. You can calculate the present value of an annuity due by multiplying the value calculated for an ordinary annuity by one plus the interest rate. A **Perpetuity** *is an infinite-lived annuity.* By multiplying the PV by the required rate of return, *i*, the perpetual cash flow can be calculated.

- As interest is compounded more frequently than once a year, both (a) the future value for a given holding period and (b) the **Effective Annual Rate** of interest will increase. This is because the more frequently interest is compounded, the greater the quantity of money accumulated and reinvested as the principal value. In situations of intra-year compounding, the actual rate of interest is greater than the stated rate of interest. **Continuous Compounding** *assumes interest will be compounded an infinite number of times per year, at intervals of microseconds.* Continuous compounding of a given deposit at a given rate of interest results in the largest value when compared to any other compounding period. The **Nominal Annual Rate** *is the contractual rate that is quoted to the borrower by the lender.* The **Effective Annual Rate,** *sometimes called the true rate, is the actual rate that is paid by the borrower to the lender.* The difference between the two rates is due to the compounding of interest at a frequency greater than once per year.

  APR is the **Annual Percentage Rate** *and is required by "truth-in-lending laws" to be disclosed to consumers. This rate is calculated by multiplying the periodic rate by the number of periods in one year.* The periodic rate is the nominal rate over the shortest time in which interest is compounded. The **APY**, or **Annual Percentage Yield,** *is the effective rate of interest that must be disclosed to consumers by banks on their savings products as a result of the "truth-in-savings laws."* These laws result in both favorable and unfavorable information to consumers. The good news is that rate quotes on both loans and savings are standardized among financial institutions. The negative is that the APR, or lending rate, is a nominal rate, while the APY, or saving rate, is an effective rate. These rates are the same when compounding occurs only once per year.

- Amortizing a loan into equal annual payments involves finding the future payments whose *present value* at the loan interest rate just equals the amount of the initial principal borrowed. Amortizing a loan involves creating an annuity out of a present amount. Then, each loan payment is allocated into the interest component and principal component. The end-of-year principal is calculated for every year and the subsequent allocation of interest and principal are calculated based on the previous year's end-of-year principal. As the principal is reduced, the interest component declines, leaving a larger portion of each subsequent loan payment to repay the principal.

Questions for Thought:

Why do we want to save money?

Why do we want to save money today instead of tomorrow?

Why do you think people will pay more for money today?

All of these questions lead to the idea of the time value of money. The time value of money is a concept that describes why money today is worth more than money tomorrow. The principle rests on the fact that one can put money into an investment that will yield interest over time. For example, someone needs money to start a business that will give a 10% return on investment. Because of this, they are willing to pay someone else interest to use it now. They pay the other person 5% interest. This way those who need money to spend can do so by letting those who want to save earn money on their savings. This shows that money today is worth more than money tomorrow because the business person was willing to give up part of his return to get money today. The concept of time value of money is the idea that money available at present time is worth more than the same amount of money in the future due to its potential earning capacity. This core principle of finance holds that provided money can earn interest, any amount of money is worth more the sooner it is received. Also referred to as "present discounted value".

http://www.investopedia.com/video/play/understanding-time-value-of-money

What Is Time Value?

If you are like most people, you would choose to receive the $10,000 now. After all, three years is a long time to wait. Why would any rational person defer payment into the future when he or she could have the same amount of money now? For most of us, taking the money in the present is just plain instinctive. So at the most basic level, the time value of money demonstrates that all things being equal, it is better to have money now rather than later.

A video that gives another illustration:
http://www.investopedia.com/video/play/understanding-time-value-of-money/#axzz28jRoP97A

Time Lines

The first step in a time value analysis is to set up a timeline to help you visualize what's happening in the particular problem. To illustrate, consider the following diagram, where PV represents $100 that is in a bank account today and FV is the value that will be in the account at some future time (3 years from now in the example):

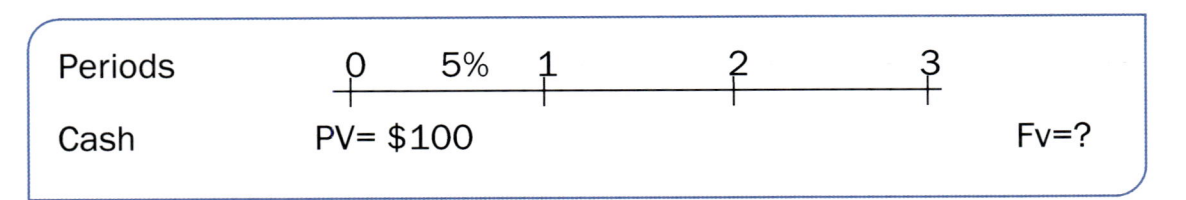

Periods	0 5% 1 2 3
Cash	PV= $100 Fv=?

The intervals from 0-1 and 1-2 are periods such as years or months. Cash flows are shown directly below the tick marks, and the relevant interest rate I shown just above the line. Unknown cash flows, which you are trying to find, are indicated by question marks. Here the interest rate is constant for all 3 years. The interest rate is generally held constant, but if it varies then in the diagram we show different rates for the different periods.

Timelines are especially important when you are first learning time value concepts, but even experts use them to analyze complex problems. Throughout this book, our procedure will be to set up a timeline to show what's happening, provide an equation that must be solved to find the answer, and then explain how to solve the equation with a regular calculator, a financial calculator, and a computer spreadsheet.

Future Values

A dollar in hand today is worth more than a dollar to be received in the future. The process of going forward from present values (PV) to future values (FVs) is called compounding. There are four different procedures to solve time value problems.

Step by Step Approach

The timeline itself can be modified and used to find the FV of $100 compounded for 3 years at 5% as shown:

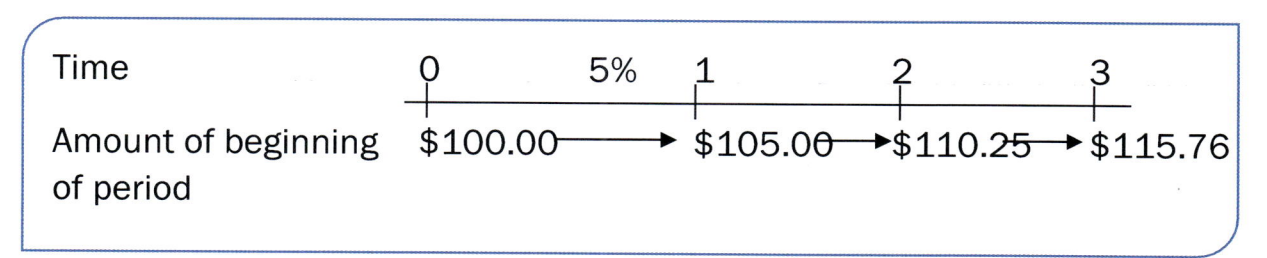

Time	0	5%	1	2	3
Amount of beginning of period	$100.00 →		$105.00 →	$110.25 →	$115.76

You can earn $100(0.05) =$5 of interest during the first year.

So the amount at the end of 1 (or at at t=1) is:

FV1=PV + INT = PV +PV (I) = PV (I +1) = $100 (1 + 0.05) = $105

The process continues and because the beginning balance is higher in each successive year, the interest earned, $15.76 is reflected in the final balance of $115.76.

The step-by-step approach is useful because it shows exactly what is happening. However, this approach is time-consuming especially if the number of years I large and you are using a calculator rather than Excel so streamlined procedures have been developed.

Formula Approach

In the step-by-step approach, we can multiply the amount at the beginning of each period by (1 +I) = (1.05). If N=3 then we multiply PV by (1+I) three different times, which is why it is the same as multiplying the beginning amount by (1+I) 3. This concept can be extended and the result is this key equation: N

$$FVn = P(1 + I)^N$$

Present Values

Finding present values is called discounting and is the opposite of compounding. If you know the PV, you know the PV you can compound to find the FV; or if you know the FV, you can discount to find the PV.

$$Compounding\ to\ find\ future\ values : \ Future\ Value = FVn = PV\ (1 + I)^N$$

$$Discounting\ to\ find\ present\ values : \ Present\ Values = PV = PV = \frac{FV_N}{(1 + I)^N}$$

To find present values you must work backward or form right to left, dividing the future value and each subsequent amount by (1+I) with the present value of $100. The step-by-step procedure shows exactly what's happening and that can be quite useful when you are working on complex problems or

> ## EXAMPLE
>
> - Joe has the option of receiving $1000 now or when his rich uncle dies.
> - If he takes the money now he can put the money in a bound that gives 8%
> - What should he do? Why?
>
> *Because money is worth more today than tomorrow we can compute a way to compare the value of money earned tomorrow compared to the value of money earned today.*
>
> *To compare $10,000 received today to $10,000 received today we need to look at the interest that is given up. We can figure the interest that is received on $10,000 if the money was put into the bank for 3 years and subtract that from the $10,000 that is to be received 3 years from now. This number will show you how much the future money is worth today. See the figure below.*

trying to explain a model to others. However, it is inefficient, especially if you are dealing with more than a year or two.

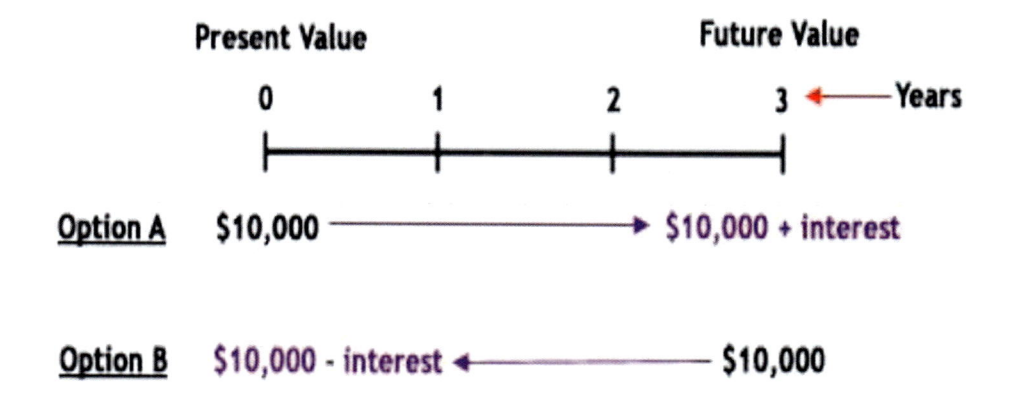

```
                Present Value                Future Value
                     0          1         2        3  ←— Years
                     ├──────────┼─────────┼────────┤

   Option A       $10,000  ─────────────────────→  $10,000 + interest

   Option B       $10,000 - interest  ←───────────  $10,000
```

66 Financial Analysis and Time Value of Money

Another way to find present value is to take the amount of money being received in the future and divide it by one plus the forgone interest rate or...

$$PV = FV \frac{1}{(1+r)^n}$$

$FV = Future\ Value$
$r = rate\ of\ return$
$n = number\ of\ periods$

PROBLEM

Find the present value of $10,000 received 5 years from now.

One can use present value to compare money received today to money received tomorrow.

Future Value

Future value can be used to calculate how much money received to today will be worth tomorrow. In other words, it is a way to calculate how much your money will be worth if it is earning interest. The equation for this is very simple. It is as follows,

$$FV = PV \times (1+r)^n$$

$PV = Present\ Value$
$r = rate\ of\ return$
$n = number\ of\ periods$

PROBLEM

Find the future value of $10,000 it is deposited in an interest bearing account yielding 5% interest.

Annuities

Annuities are a stream of payment received over a certain time.

If payments occur at the end of each period, then we have an ordinary annuity. Payments on mortgages, car loans, and student loans are generally made at the ends of the periods and thus are ordinary annuities. If the payments are made at the beginning of each period, then we have an annuity due.

Future Value of an Ordinary Annuity

Consider ordinary annuity whose time line was shown previously, where you deposit $100 at the end of each year for 3 years and earn 5% per year. Here's how to calculate Future value of annuity or FVAn, using the same approaches as for single cash flows.

Inputs							
Payment amount =	PMT =	($100.00)					
Interest Rate =	I =	5.00%					
No. of Periods =	N =	3					

1. Step by Step			0	1	2	3	
				($100)	($100)	($100)	
Multiply each payment by (1+I)N-t and sum these FVs to find FVAn						$100 $105.00 $110.25 315	

| 2. Formula: | | | | | | | |
| | FVAn = | ((1+I)n/I) - (1/I) | | = | | 315.25 | |

3. Financial Calculator:			3	5	$0	($100.00)	
			N	I/YR	PV	PMT	FV
							315.25

Financial Analysis and Time Value of Money

Future Value of an Annuity Due

Because each payment occurs one period earlier with annuity due, the payments will all earn interest for one additional period. Therefore, the FV of an annuity due will be greater than that of a similar ordinary annuity.

If you went through the step-by-step procedure, you would see that the annuity due has a FV of $331.01 vs $315.25 for an ordinary annuity. We can calculate the annuity due by using the formula:

$$FVA_{due} = FVA_{ordinary}(1 + I)$$

And then we can solve this by plugging the function into a calculator and it would look like this:

Inputs: 3 (N), 5 (I/YR), 0 (PV), - (PMT), FV

Outputs: 331.01

Finding Annuities Payments, Periods, and Interest Rates

Finding annuity payments, PMT:

We need to accumulate $10,000 and have it available 5 years from now. We can earn 6% on our money. Thus we know that FV = $10,000, PV =0, N=5, and I/YR = 6. Here's how you can plug this example into your calculator to find the PMT:

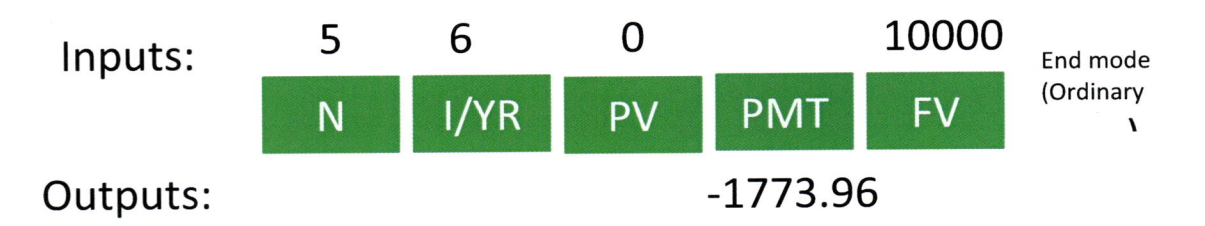

Inputs: 5 (N), 6 (I/YR), 0 (PV), PMT, 10000 (FV)

End mode (Ordinary)

Outputs: -1773.96

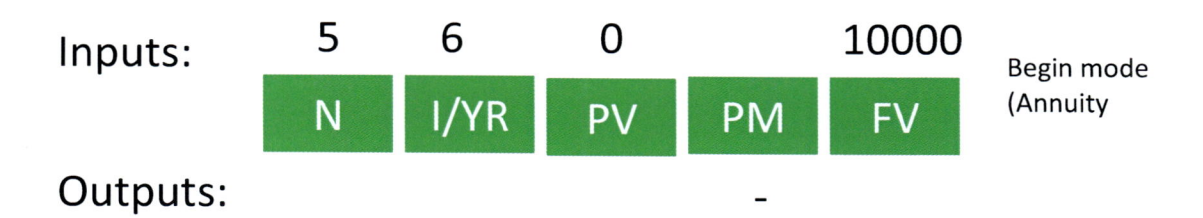

Inputs:	5	6	0		10000	Begin mode (Annuity
	N	I/YR	PV	PM	FV	

Outputs: -

Thus you must put away $1,773.96 per year if you make payments at the end of each year, but only $1,673.55 if the payments begin immediately. Finally, not that the required payment for the annuity due is the ordinary annuity payment divided by (1+I): $1,773.96/1.06=$1,673.55.

Finding the Number of Periods, N:

Suppose you decide to make end-of-year deposits, but you can save only $1,200 per year. Again assuming that you would earn 6%, how long would it take you to reach your $10,000 goal? Here is the calculator setup:

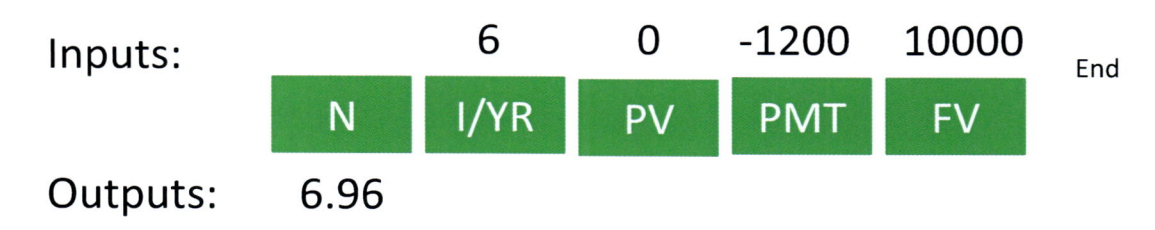

Inputs:		6	0	-1200	10000	End
	N	I/YR	PV	PMT	FV	

Outputs: 6.96

Finding Interest Rate, I:

Now suppose you can save only $1,200 annually, but you still need to have the $10,000 in 5 years. What rate of return would you have to earn to reach your goal? Here is the calculator setup:

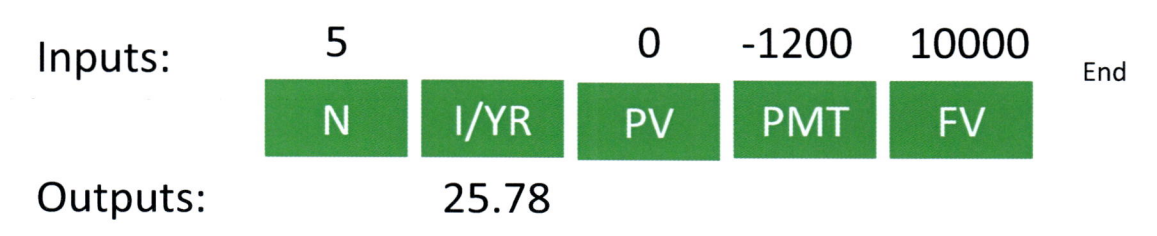

Inputs:	5		0	-1200	10000	End
	N	I/YR	PV	PMT	FV	

Outputs: 25.78

Finding the Interest Rate, I

Thus far we have used equations to find the future and present values. Those equations have four variables, and if we know three of them, then we can solve for the fourth. Thus if we know PV, I, and N we can solve for FV, or if we know FV, I and N we can solve to find PV. Now suppose we know PV, FV, and N, and we want to find I. For example, suppose we know that given security has a cost of $100 and that it will return $150 after 10 years. Thus we know PV, FV, and N and we want to find the rate of return we will earn if we buy the security. Here's the solution:

$FV = PV(1+I)^N : \$150 = \$100 (1+I)^{10} : \$150/\$100 = (1+I)^{10} : (1+I)^{10} = 1.5$
$: (1+I) = 1.5^{(\frac{1}{10})} : 1 + I = 1.0414 : I = 0.141 = 4.14\%$

Finding the Number of Years, N

Sometimes it is important to know how long it will take to accumulate a specific sum of money, given the beginning sum of money and the rate at which it will earn. For example, suppose we now have $500,000 and the interest rate is 4.5%. How long will it be before we have $1 million dollars?

$$\$1,000,000 = \$500,000(1 + 0.045)^N$$

We need to solve for N, and we can use three procedures: a financial calculator, Excel or by working the natural logs. We recommend a calculator. Here's what it would look like:

Inputs:	N	4.5 I/YR	-50000 PV	0 PMT	100000 FV

Outputs: 15.7473

Perpetuities

A consol, or **Perpetuity**, *is simply an annuity whose promised payments extend out forever.* Since the payments go on forever, you can't apply the step-by-step approach. However, it's easy to find the PV of a perpetuity with the following formula:

$$PV\ of\ perpetuity = \frac{PMT}{I}$$

Uneven or Irregular Cash Flow

The definition of an annuity includes the term constant payment—in other words; annuities involve a set of identical payments over a given number of periods. Although many financial decisions do involve constant payments, many others involve cash flows that are uneven or irregular. There are two important classes of uneven cash flows:

1. Those in which the cash flow stream consists of a series of annuity payments plus an additional final lump sum in Year N
2. All other uneven streams

Bongs are instances of the first type while stocks and capital investments illustrate the second kind.

Future Value of an Uneven Cash Flow Stream

The future value of an uneven cash flow stream (Sometimes called the terminal, or horizon, value) is found by compounding each payment to the end of the stream and then summing the future values:

$$FV = CF_0(1+I)^N + CF_1(1+I)^{N-1} + CF_2(1+I)^{N-2)} + \ldots + CF_{N-1}(1+I)$$
$$+ CF_N = \sum_{t=0}^{N} CF_t(1+I)^{N-t}$$

Growing Annuities

Normally an annuity is defined as a series of constant payments to be received over a specified number of periods. However, the term growing annuity is used to describe a series of payments that grow at a constant rate.

EXAMPLE 1: Finding a Constant Real Income

Growing annuities are often used in the area of financial planning, where a prospective retiree wants to determine the maximum constant real or inflation-adjusted withdrawals that he or she can make over a specified number of years. To calculate this using a calculator we would use the formula:

$$Real\ Rate = r_r = [(1 + r_{NOM})/(1 + Inflation)] - 1.0$$

EXAMPLE: Initial Deposit to Accumulate a Future Sum

As another example of growing annuities, suppose you need to accumulate $100,000 in 10 years. You plan to make a deposit in a bank now, at Time 0, and then make 9 more deposits at the beginning of each of the following 9 years, for a total of 10 deposits. The bank pays 6% interest, you expect inflation to be 2% per year, and you plan to increase your annual deposits at the inflation rate. How much must you deposit initially? The first step is to calculate the real rate:

$$Real\ Rate = r_r = [1.06/1.02] - 1.0 = 0.0392157 = 3.9215686\ \%$$

Next, since inflation is expected to be 2% per year, in 10 years the target $100,000 will have a real value of:

$$\$100,000/(1 + 0.02)^{10} = \$82,034.83$$

Now we can find the size of the required initial payment by setting a financial calculator to the BEGIN MODE and then putting the appropriate numbers in their functions. The key to this analysis is to express I/YR, FV, and PMT in real, not nominal terms.

Internet Video: http://www.investopedia.com/video/play/understanding-an-annuity/#axzz29QHw7Axi

The present value of an annuity can be calculated by finding the present value of each payment received over the life cycle. For example:

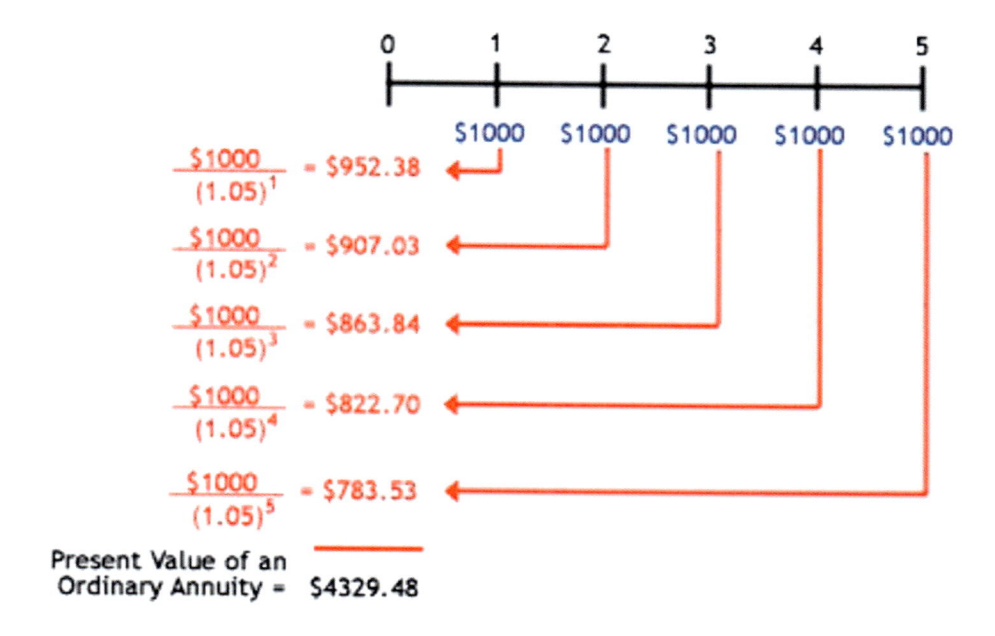

$$\frac{\$1000}{(1.05)^1} = \$952.38$$

$$\frac{\$1000}{(1.05)^2} = \$907.03$$

$$\frac{\$1000}{(1.05)^3} = \$863.84$$

$$\frac{\$1000}{(1.05)^4} = \$822.70$$

$$\frac{\$1000}{(1.05)^5} = \$783.53$$

Present Value of an Ordinary Annuity = $4329.48

The future value of an annuity is found by computing the future value of each cash flow invested over a life cycle. For example...

74 Financial Analysis and Time Value of Money

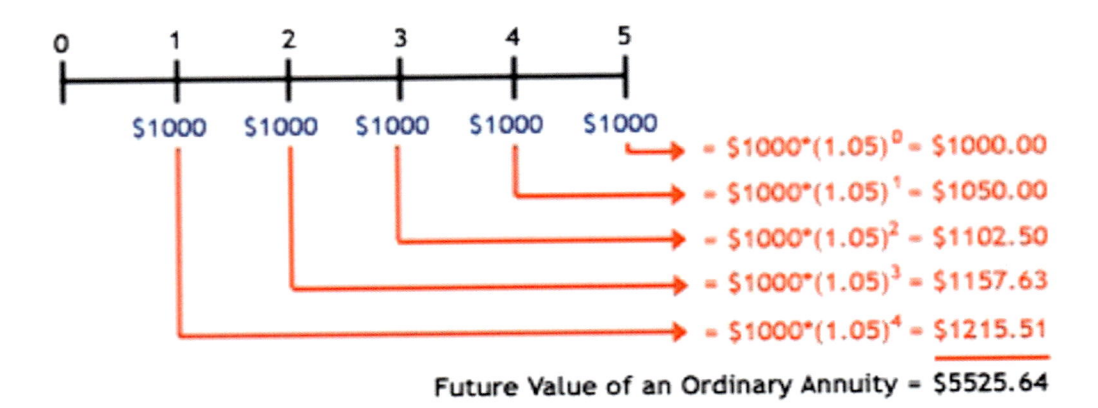

```
0     1       2       3       4       5
|-----|-------|-------|-------|-------|
    $1000  $1000   $1000   $1000   $1000
```

- $\$1000 \cdot (1.05)^0 = \$1000.00$
- $\$1000 \cdot (1.05)^1 = \$1050.00$
- $\$1000 \cdot (1.05)^2 = \$1102.50$
- $\$1000 \cdot (1.05)^3 = \$1157.63$
- $\$1000 \cdot (1.05)^4 = \$1215.51$

Future Value of an Ordinary Annuity = $5525.64

PROBLEM

Find the future value of $4,000 invested for three years, $3,000, invested for two years, and $2,000 invested for one year.

Amortization Tables

Amortization tables are used to show a stream of payments made over the life of a loan. A table will show how much someone must pay each month for the life of the loan. It will also, show how much of each payment will be interest and how much will be principle.

Internet Video: http://www.investopedia.com/video/play/amortization/#axzz29QHw7Axi

Here is an example of an amortization table:

Month	Amount	Amount After Interest	Payment	Interest Part	Principle Part	New Amount
1	5000	5052.083333	445.4143	52.08333333	393.3309802	4606.66902
2	4606.66902	4654.655155	445.4143	47.98613562	397.4281779	4209.240842
3	4209.240842	4253.087101	445.4143	43.84625877	401.5680548	3807.672787
4	3807.672787	3847.336045	445.4143	39.6632582	405.7510554	3401.921732
5	3401.921732	3437.358416	445.4143	35.43668471	409.9776288	2991.944103
6	2991.944103	3023.110187	445.4143	31.1660844	414.2482291	2577.695874
7	2577.695874	2604.546872	445.4143	26.85099868	418.5633149	2159.132559
8	2159.132559	2181.623523	445.4143	22.49096415	422.9233494	1736.209209
9	1736.209209	1754.294722	445.4143	18.0855126	427.328801	1308.880408
10	1308.880408	1322.514579	445.4143	13.63417092	431.7801426	877.1002659
11	877.1002659	886.236727	445.4143	9.136461103	436.2778525	440.8224134
12	440.8224134	445.4143136	445.4143	4.59190014	440.8224134	2.18279E-11

Application: discuss how one would use it when planning to take out and loan and how it would be used in a personal budget.

> **ACTIVITY**
>
> Activity: Go to http://www.amortizationtable.org/ or other internet source and have students create an amortization table for either there current loan or a hypothetical one.

4: Conclusion

This book covers financial analysis and time value of money. Financial analysis is the process of evaluating personal funds, businesses, projects, budgets, and other finance-related transactions to determine their performance and suitability. Typically, financial analysis is used to analyze whether an entity is stable, solvent, liquid, or profitable enough to warrant a monetary investment. To get a good understanding of personal finance, several financial ratios are used and compared with some type of benchmark that indicates the financial condition of the person or company. If conducted internally, financial analysis can help managers make future business decisions or review historical trends for past successes. If conducted externally, financial analysis can help investors choose the best possible investment opportunities.

The time value of money (TVM) is the concept that the money you have now is worth more than the identical sum in the future due to its potential earning capacity. This core principle of finance holds that provided money can earn interest, any amount of money is worth more the sooner it is received. TVM is also sometimes referred to as present discounted value. Time value of money is based on the idea that people would rather have money today than in the future. Given that money can earn compound interest, it is more valuable in the present rather than the future. The formula for computing time value of money consider the payment now, the future value, the interest rate, and the time frame. The number of compounding periods during each time frame is an important determinant in the time value of money formula as well.

Videos for Financial Analysis

Use the following videos to apply what you have learned in this book

What is a balance sheet? Balance sheet definition and examples

https://www.youtube.com/watch?v=NkbCHQKxXXY

1.) How many parts is a balance sheet divided up in?

2.) What are the parts that make up a balance sheet?

3.) What does the asset section consist of?

4.) What is the liability and equity section?

The Income Statement defined and explained

https://www.youtube.com/watch?v=-bUSEls5Y

1.) What is an income statement?

2.) What are the different types of income statements?

3.) How is an income statement divided up?

4.) What is included in an income statement?

Cash Flow Statement explained

https://www.youtube.com/watch?v=mZBjsIYrLvM

1.) How does a cash flow statement work?

2.) How do cash balance and cash flow relate to each other?

3.) What are cash flow from operating activities, cash flow from investing activities, and cash flow from financing activities?

4.) What is a good metaphor to see the cash balance?

Basic Financial Statements

https://www.youtube.com/watch?v=B7300KsDdYY

1.) What is a financial statement?

2.) How many financial statements are there?

3.) What are the types of financial statements?

References

Investopedia – Educating the world about finance. (n.d.). *Investopedia – Educating the world about finance*. Retrieved October 15, 2012, from http://www.investopedia.com

Phillips, F., Libby, R., & Libby, P. A. (2011). *Fundamentals of financial accounting* (3rd ed.). Boston: McGraw-Hill Irwin.

http://www.thecorys.com/babs/key_financial_ratios.htm

http://www.thefrugaltoad.com/personalfinance/personal-financial-ratios-everyone-should-know

http://www.investopedia.com

http://www.investopedia.com/articles/03/082703.asp#axzz28mUD3tte

http://www.investopedia.com/terms/t/timevalueofmoney.asp#axzz28mUD3tte

http://www.investopedia.com/university/ratios/liquidity-measurement/ratio1.asp#ixzz28olvdszh

http://www.investopedia.com/university/ratios/liquidity-measurement/ratio2.asp#ixzz28omb7UFG

http://www.sba.gov/sites/default/files/tools_sbf_finasst413_0.pdf

http://management.about.com/cs/money/a/CostBenefit_2.htm

www.investopedia.com/university/ratios/

"Business Finance." *Introduction to Risk and Return -*. N.p., n.d. Web. 02 Oct. 2012. <http://www.gaebler.com/Introduction-to-Risk-and-Return.htm>.

"Expected Return." *Expected Return*. N.p., n.d. Web. 02 Oct. 2012. <http://www.zenwealth.com/BusinessFinanceOnline/RR/ExpectedReturn.html>.

"Measures of Risk - Variance and Standard Deviation." *Measures of Risk - Variance and Standard Deviation*. N.p., n.d. Web. 02 Oct. 2012. <http://www.zenwealth.com/BusinessFinanceOnline/RR/MeasuresOfRisk.html>.

"Risk and Return." *Risk and Return*. N.p., n.d. Web. 02 Oct. 2012. <http://www.zenwealth.com/BusinessFinanceOnline/RR/RiskAndReturn.html>.

Made in United States
Orlando, FL
09 June 2024

47665406R00044